CW01646568

Adventures With Orkney Uncovered

Kinlay Francis

Copyright © 2024 by Kinlay Francis

Illustrations Copyright © 2024 by Lesley Francis

First Published 2024 by Orkney Uncovered

Paperback ISBN: 978-1-0687590-0-0

eBook ISBN: 978-1-0687590-1-7

All rights reserved.

No portion of this book may be reproduced in any form without written permission from the publisher or author.

Disclaimer:

In my anecdotes, I have not used the real names or identities of my tour guests or people I have encountered on my walks, or accounts from others in the Orkney tourist industry. Many of the scenes are fictionalised re-creations of actual events and I have added an air of creativity to the stories to give them more flair. The historical and factual information in my book is correct to the best of my knowledge.

For my Benjamin

Contents

Foreword

To meet Kinlay is indeed to meet a real-life Viking, or at least the closest modern-day ancestry you are likely to find. Were he not guiding on Orkney he would surely have plenty of work as a Hollywood extra. Kinlay is also a great friend of the Royal Navy Mine Clearance Diving Branch. Every year, Clearance Divers from the Royal Navy dive on the wreck of HMS ROYAL OAK in Scapa Flow, replacing the old ensign with a new one to honour the 835 men and boys who died when she was sunk in 1939. Kinlay co-ordinates events and looks after the divers, showing the finest of Orkney welcomes. He draws together the history, geography and culture of these wonderful islands, and as a host is second to none.

I first met Kinlay at a Royal Navy Diving Branch dinner at Horsea Island, where we collectively hosted friends of the branch to thank them for their support. It was immediately clear that he was larger-than-life both in stature and personality.

Not only does Kinlay's bloodline go back to actual Viking

warriors, he is a true Orcadian with a deep understanding of the geography, history, people and spirit of these beautiful and mystical islands. His knowledge and passion are deep-rooted and his personality truly brings that knowledge and passion to life, making him the perfect companion to learn about the real Orkney.

Working as a guide on Orkney, Kinlay meets people from every corner of the globe; from every religion, country, colour and creed, and often very different cultures and places. This inevitably leads to colourful, and often amusing, scenarios. While roaring with laughter over a dram or in a gale about some of his anecdotes, many of Kinlay's clients have implored him to put his experiences into writing. During the Covid pandemic when he was temporarily forced to take a sabbatical, Kinlay began to do just this, and put some of his stories onto paper.

This book is the culmination of that endeavour, and provides a light-hearted look at some of the more amusing interplays during Kinlay's many years of guiding.

Easy to pick up and read from any point, this entertaining read will transport you for a short time to the beautiful Orkney archipelago, as if being shown the sights by the big man himself. Pop the kettle on or pour a wee dram, and settle down to enjoy - and indeed be educated in- some of the more humorous and curious elements of Orcadian life.

Commander Keith Mabbott Royal Navy (Rtd)

About the author

Kinlay Francis

Summer 2023.

My name is Kinlay and I own and operate *Orkney Uncovered*, a private tour company, with my wife Kirsty. We have a delightful and amusing son named Benjamin, who is nine, and a furry wee beastie called Holly, our yellow Labrador. We are big advocates of the great outdoors, and Orkney is a massive outdoor adventure playground for all ages.

For many years I have guided countless people, unicorns and toy puffins from around the globe throughout Orkney, our beautiful archipelago of 70 islands. To break the ice I often tell my guests an amusing story about questions I've been asked as a guide and a local. I have often been asked by clients, friends and family to write a book of these funny anecdotes and tales – so here it is. I hope that anyone reading it can have a good laugh and let it brighten your day, as let's face it, we all need cheering up from time and time, and laughter is the best medicine there is.

Lesley Francis

Lesley a listed and well-known watercolour artist inspired by seascapes and landscapes both in Orkney and around the globe. She also works in Japanese inks and has many produced acclaimed works inspired by the Art Deco period.

This is the first time she has attempted light-hearted sketches, and she hopes they will bring a smile to the reader.

The watercolour sketches in this book are solely based on her imagination set in the Orkney landscapes and relate to incidents in Kinlay's anecdotes.

Chapter 1

Orkney Weather

One of the most common questions we get asked by prospective clients is what they will need to wear to survive the weather. 'Wear appropriate clothes,' I answer. The question always makes me laugh, as it is a myth that the further North you go the colder it gets. Orkney is blessed with the North Atlantic Drift, a warm weather current that is pushed into the West coast by the Gulf Stream from the North Atlantic Ocean. So, throughout the year it is mild and on average between around 8°C – 15°C.

Orkney Thong – I did a tour for two sisters who arrived by cruise ship, suitably under-dressed for the local weather. I asked them if they had any proper footwear, to which they answered "We are only wearing thongs today." The shock and red face on myself sent them overboard with laughter, as they explained that the women's 'thong' in Australia is a type of sandal, not a pair of underpants. What a great way to break the ice!

Always wear appropriate clothing while touring Orkney!

Russian Summer - A number of years ago I picked up a group of Russians from a private jet. It was July, and a hot day around 26°C. They disembarked the aircraft donned in what I can only describe as 'arctic survival gear'. It was a surreal experience seeing a bunch of lads approaching me, visibly sweating, wearing a variety of thick down coats, woolly hats, salopettes, thick mitts and mountaineering boots. These chaps had flown in from St Petersburg, which interestingly enough is roughly the same latitude as Orkney at around 59 degrees North. The main man, Yuri, who is now a personal friend of mine, commented that his pilot had told him that Orkney has savage weather throughout the year. At the bequest of his fellow friends they had made a stop to Aberdeen airport to go outdoor gear shopping, before jumping back on board their jet and heading to Orkney dressed as abominable snowmen.

Yuri, who found this hilarious, shook my hand, made an about turn, said something in high-tempo Russian to his embarrassed pilot and friends, goose-stepped back to the plane and emerged 10 minutes later dressed in shorts and t-shirt, with his friends in tow. The pilot waved from the plane, looking like he had been hauled over the proverbial coals. It was a superb tour, the highlight of the day being the picnic whilst sunbathing at the Bay of Skaill.

Food Shortages - My favourite Orkney weather-related question from a client came after we had driven all around Orkney Mainland: "How do you survive the winter months? Do you have to slaughter your own animals?" To which I responded,

"No, we go to Tesco!"

Orkney Sasquatch - During winter we have a shooting season for Greylag Geese. They are lovely to look at, but due to our milder climate their numbers have rapidly increased over the last twenty years. To keep their numbers down and to stop them destroying our grass crop, they are culled within strict quotas.

In a cold December a few years back, I took a chap on tour who had come here to shoot the geese, but also brought a special kind of licence with him. His question stills makes me laugh to this day: "Can you show me where I can hunt the Sasquatch?"

Despite my valiant efforts to explain that we have very small wooded areas, and that Bigfoot was likely a myth, this chap was determined to bag and tag one.

The Umbrella - I hope anyone reading this who is due to come to Orkney will heed my warning. Umbrellas - or Brollies, as we call them - will NOT work in the Northern Isles! In fact, they can be more of a danger than anything else.

Umbrellas don't work in the strong Orkney Winds

Many times I have warned travellers, especially from cruise ships, that their umbrellas will fail almost instantly here in

Orkney.

One woman from a visiting cruise ship wanted to prove me wrong and went to great lengths to claim that her brolly, which was crafted from carbon fibre, would survive the strength of the Orkney winds. As we hiked along the path to the Ring of Brodgar, sure enough it started pelting down. I simply put my hood up, as did her husband, who said he loved the "crap" weather as it reminded him of home in Michigan. The woman, who shall remain nameless, struggled with her brolly. I even offered her some assistance, but that was flatly refused.

And so, her husband and I kept walking and chatting about the ancient marvel ahead of us.

As we reached the entrance of the Henge, now with a strong head wind as well as rhe rain, we heard a screech. We looked back and to our amusement his wife was airborne and being pulled majestically across the wet, soggy field like a herd of Bison charging across the Great Plains. To make matters worse we could hear thunder rumbling, so carbon fibre might have been a bit of an issue. As luck would have it the lady needn't have worried, as said brolly had not only become inverted but had also snapped. As we approached the bedraggled edition of Mary Poppins, her husband was about to say something when she looked directly into his eyes and cried out,

"Don't you say a word!"

The best thing about having my hood zipped up was that

it hid my tears of laughter!

Reinforced carbon fibre umbrellas usually don't work either!

Low Tide - A number of years ago I arrived to pick up a client from an excellent B&B, and while waiting I witnessed a couple complaining about the sea view. The problem appeared to be that they couldn't actually *see* the sea, while the brochure said the accommodation had a sea view - which it does. You simply open your eyes and look at the sea. The well-mannered accommodation provider patiently explained that the tide was out, to which the couple responded, "Well is it coming *back*?"

Don't worry. The tide always goes out and always comes back again.

Other funny winter and weather-related Qs:

Does the island close during winter?

Kinlay, why is it raining?

Do the Vikings raid the islands in winter?

Do the local people go into hibernation?

Do icebreakers have to resupply the islands?

Do you live underground during winter?

Do you need to wear animal skins to survive in winter?

Do you have implants for your eyes to make it lighter? – this is my favourite!

How do you transport a generator to the island?

Are you resupplied by helicopters?

Are you stalked by wolves during winter?

In which direction are the Northern Lights (also known as the Aurora Borealis)?

The Northern Lights can be seen in the North, as the name suggests.

There are so many weather-related questions that I have only included a select few. I am sure many other guides and accommodation providers have heard some classics too.

Chapter 2

Random Questions, Requests and Outbursts

Orkney is much like anywhere else that's popular with visitors, and we too get asked random, and sometimes hilarious, questions.

Several years years ago I was walking through Princes St Gardens in Edinburgh, when a gentleman stopped me dead in my tracks and asked, "Hey you, what time does the one o' clock gun fire?" I answered with a smile,

"Two o'clock."

The following are just a few of the of my favourite questions, requests and outbursts here in Orkney.

Spence or is it, Pence? - On a warm summer's day in 2018 I was guiding a lovely family around the Cathedral, and as I was answering some questions about the Norse stone mason marks we were rudely interrupted by someone stating that the gravestone 'Spence' next to us was named after their Vice President Mike Pence. I politely explained that they were mistaken, and the gravestone in fact dated back to the early 17th C and as far as I was aware, Vice President Pence was not several hundred years old. As I turned back to my clients, the person shouted at me that I was wrong, and that a shop outside the Cathedral was called Pence's. I responded by saying, "It's the Orkney surname Spence, and it's missing the 'S' because the weather blew it off."

One of my clients had had enough by this time and pointed out to the shouting guest that there *is* a place in Orkney named after their President. The person answered, "Oh yeah, where is that?"

"Twatt," the man answered.

At this point the person went into a mini tantrum and stormed out, much to the relief of everyone. I stood, stunned, rolled my eyes and continued the tour. I have to say in my client's defence that the comeback was nothing short of priceless. I would further add that as a guide there is an unspoken rule to never mention politics unless asked, and then to answer as pragmatically as possible so as to avoid confrontation.

Viking Raid - In 2019 shortly before the Covid pandemic gripped the world, I took a lovely family from Canada on tour. As we walked past Saint Magnus Cathedral we witnessed what's known here as a 'blackening' – an explanation of which will follow, below.

As I was explaining to my tour guests about the Cathedral and its Norse stone masons, we witnessed the aforementioned blackening, driving past. Suddenly there came screams from a woman and her husband, who threw themselves to the ground.

Concerned, I ran over and asked what had happened and if they needed assistance. The couple quickly responded saying that they didn't want the Vikings to kill them. I tried my very best to explain to this couple that the Viking Ages ended in 1066 at the Battle of Stamford Bridge, and I didn't think Vikings had cars back then either. The man looked blankly at me, then cried, "Don't hurt us, you look like a Viking!"

Yes!!! At last! I thanked the man, who had made my day!

And so it was that my alter ego name became *Kinlay the Viking*. I do, after all, have a large percentage of my DNA from the Swedish Varangian Vikings who fought as elite guards for the Byzantine Empire.

It's traditional. But did its origin really start in Viking times??

History behind the blackening: this is an Orkney tradition whereby a bride- and groom-to-be are kidnapped by their friends for the day, covered in treacle, flour, feathers etc, tied to either the Mercat Cross outside the Cathedral or the road sign in the middle of the Kiln Corner roundabout and left there until released by their friends and family. The tradition has several variations but the idea is that the groom and bride are washed after the blackening, and are therefore clean for their future together. This is the version I was told, anyway.

The blackening can go on for hours, and usually the victim is driven around on the back of a truck, covered in treacle, with the kidnappers having a great time bashing drums and causing what the local Sheriff describes as 'an acceptable breach of the peace'.

Local to the Rescue – During the winter of 2022 I was heading over to the Brough of Birsay with a client when we were intercepted by what can be only described as two 'creatures' from the black lagoon. Sorry, I mean 'over-ly-geared-up twitchers', aka bird watchers. As they trudged towards us in multiple layers and legions of optics, we stood aside to let them past. As. She passed me the woman snapped, "Are you a local?" to which I nodded.

The lady was in a distressed state, and with flapping hands indicated towards an area on the beach. "We think there is a dead seal over there, can you please call someone to remove it?"

I replied that there are many dead seals on the Orkney shores, as unfortunately the rough seas can kill new pups, which end up on the shore, but that the high tides will likely take the carcass back out to sea.

The older woman, a visitor to the island along with her husband, then said, "As a local you should know who to speak to. As its head is missing, we think it might be dead!"

This was exactly what they said. I simply replied,

" Yes, if its head is missing it's most probably dead."

We kept walking to avoid further unwanted confrontation.

Gulfstream G650 – A few years ago I took a phone call from a travel agent in London who enquired about her clients booking a tour. Everything seemed to be going well until she said that due to limited time, her clients wanted to do the tour from aboard their private jet.

Last time I checked, 'Orkney' - as us locals describe the 70 strong island archipelago – covers an area of 202 square miles. The cruising speed of a G650 is approximately 594 mph, and as far as I know it does not have the hovering capabilities of a F-35 Lightning or a Harrier Jump Jet.

After carefully explaining to the travel agent the speed of the Gulfstream G650 and the size of the archipelago, she asked, "Look, can you do the tour or not?" I answered that I couldn't, and hung up. Funnily enough, a friend of mine and fellow guide contacted me the following day to say that a very abrupt travel agent from London wanted to do a tour for her clients by private jet. He had laughed and hung up the call after being asked what the time zone was in the Oakley islands!

Heather on Heather – A few years ago I picked up a couple from a visiting cruise ship. The lady, who was called Heather, had one main mission: to stand on heather and have me take her photo, so she could show her friends 'Heather on Heather'.

This was one of the strangest requests I have ever received, but I was happy to oblige. The husband was on a working holiday and spent his time on his laptop, occasionally looking up at his wife and laughing with amusement as she tripped, uninjured, numerous times in the thick heather.

Unfortunately for me, one of my friends drove past and stopped to see what on earth was going on, to which I candidly explained the 'Heather on Heather' task. My friend, who shall remain nameless, then told his friends on Facebook. For the rest of the day, friends of friends, and just about everyone else it seemed, tooted their horns, waved, gestured and heckled myself and Heather, who interestingly enough didn't seem to mind all the attention.

On the way back to the ship, and after six hours of marching through peat bogs and being eaten alive by midges to find the perfect tuft of heather for Heather to stand on, I asked her *why* she wanted to do this? She explained that she had seen a video I'd posted on Facebook explaining the various types of heather on Orkney. Based on this, she had decided to make her way from California to Orkney in search of the 'elusive heather', as she put it. I took a very deep breath, braced myself and said, " You do know that the Sierra Nevada Mountain range in California has some of the most amazing white heather in the world (named Cassiope Mertensiana)?"

Silence fell over the back seat of the tour vehicle. The husband looked up from his laptop and rolled his eyes at his wife, who had just realised they had travelled over 5000 miles to come and see heather in Orkney when there was plenty of it close to where they lived. They burst out laughing at their monumental *faux pas* and said that at least they got some sort of a vacation.

Other questions:

Can we meet a Viking?

Please whistle us an Orca.

What time do the otters cross the road? (There's a sign in Kirkwall saying 'Otters crossing').

I want to have a picnic on top of the Old Man of Hoy (450ft sea stack).

A picnic on top of the Old Man of Hoy? Really?

Chapter 3

Orkney Farming

The Orkney economy is very buoyant, and Orkney regularly lists in the national newspapers as one of the best places to live in the UK. This is mainly due to our fertile lands for farming and many other sectors including North Sea oil, tourism, fishing and renewable energy.

Approximately 9% of the working population are employed in agriculture. Farming is the backbone of the Orkney economy. My ancestors, the Vikings, also found our rich soils to be perfect for farming. So here are a few interesting statements and questions I have fielded about farming.

Dark Ages - In my first year of trading I did a tour for a family who were interested in ancient Orkney. As we drove towards Skara Brae the teenager in the party, a 14 year old lad, asked me to stop, as he had seen something strange in the grassland. I pulled over and asked him what he was looking at. He pointed to a cow and asked, "What is it?" Dumbstruck and not sure if he was being serious, I replied,

"That's a dairy cow, where we get our milk." The lad answered, "You guys must live in the Dark Ages. Where we live, we get our milk from cartons."

Does chocolate milk come from brown cows ? Huh?!

Cattle Whisperer - In 2016 I took a couple from the Southern Hemisphere to the island of Hoy for a tour. Whilst walking to the Old Man of Hoy, I turned to see the man making strange noises to the cattle in the field. I asked if everything was OK, to which he replied that he was a professional cattle whisperer. I looked back at the man's wife, who nodded and smiled. Jim, as we shall call him, explained that, like Crocodile Dundee, he could do special animal calls and they would approach. At this point I thought I was the dafty being taken for a ride, so I laughed. My laugh was short-lived, as to my utter astonishment his strange sounds had the cattle running over one by one to meet him. Both his wife and I were in a trance and couldn't quite believe what we were seeing. Jim turned round smugly and said 'I told you so'. It was a surreal experience and a memorable one at that!

Flying Sheep – Fairly recently I was doing a tour for a family of four adults in wild weather. We had been in Birsay to watch the massive waves battering the coastline from the storm. As we travelled back towards Kirkwall one of the family pointed out a police van with its blue lights flashing. We slowed down, and I stopped alongside the police vehicle to them if everything was OK. The officer replied, "We are parked here, as the sheep from the field are flying on to the road and we are trying to put them back." I wished them luck and drove on carefully.

Around two minutes later, a question was fielded from the back of the tour vehicle that went along these lines: "What breed of sheep do you have that can fly, and can we stop to video them to put on YouTube?" I laughed out loud, to which the eldest member of the family said, "We are being serious."

I stopped at a layby and explained that there was no such thing as flying sheep and that the police officer was merely referring to the sheep being blown on to the road by the very high wind speeds (over 80 mph). The family, I think, saw 'tumbleweeds' and were genuinely upset that there were no flying sheep.

In their 'tumbleweed moment', perhaps the family detected 'wings' on said sheep.

Cardboard cut-out – In 2019 I was guiding a group of six private clients around Skaill House and grounds. As we approached the entrance to the house, one of the clients asked, "Why do you have a cardboard cut-out of a bull?"

I looked over and could see a Black Angus bull standing still in the field looking across the entrance to Skaill House. I explained that it was a real bull. One of the clients was convinced otherwise, and felt it needed further investigation.

As we parked the tour vehicle the person in question got out and made a beeline for the field. At this point both I and the rest of the party shouted for the person not to go into the field, as said cardboard cut-out had moved from its original position.

The person - who shall remain nameless - chose not to heed our warnings, climbed over the gate and marched into the field. Mr Cardboard cut-out had other ideas and started to use his prowess and stomp the ground. The person could be heard shouting a number of expletives whilst making a very sharp exit towards the gate. In fact, I have never seen anyone climb up and over a gate so fast! There was a barrage of laughter, clapping and heckling from the rest of the group.

Mr Cardboard cut-out, cool as a cucumber walked back to its original position and stood still for the next victim to fall foul of his dastardly plot.

Never go wandering into a field with a bull!

Other farm-related questions:

We want to chase a flock of sheep.

Can we try cow tipping?

Kinlay, how can you tell it's a bull?

Does chocolate milk come from brown cattle? (See Dark Ages section.)

Can we pick some barley to make a sandwich?

Chapter 4

58.8 Degrees North

Orkney lies at 58.8 degrees North, approximately the same latitude as Stockholm, in Sweden, and St Petersburg, in Russia. Unlike these countries we don't get hot summers and severe winters. This is due to the North Atlantic Drift from our prevailing westerly, which I mentioned in Chapter 1.

Orkney, along with our neighbour Shetland, are called the Northern Isles of Scotland, not the Western Isles, which I will return to shortly.

While we are on this subject, we also have a Norse heritage. Both Orkney and Shetland were gifted as part of a marriage dowry between King Christian I of Denmark, Norway and Sweden to King James III of Scotland in 1469. We were under Norwegian rule until 1611. We feel proud of our Scandinavian history.

We don't all play the Bagpipes, nor do we all wear kilts. Kilts are mostly worn for military events and weddings. Even our flag resembles a mixture of the Norwegian and Danish flags.

The Compass – In June 2013 I was walking with a couple who had travelled from the far West of the United States. The husband asked me to show him a map so he could see where we were. I was very pleased to meet someone who loves charts and OS maps as much as I do. I indicated to the gentleman that we were looking towards the North Sea. At this point the chap then asked me, "How do you find North on a compass?"

I offered him the compass, and with it in hand he walked around in circles. I then showed him North, to which he asked the question, "Thank you. Now how do I get to the South?"

I replied, "Turn your body 180 degrees."

He didn't believe me so I moved his body, complete with compass, a full 180'.

Edinburgh Castle - By far one of the funniest things I have ever witnessed was a gentleman and his family charging down the gangplank of the Caribbean Princess cruise ship dressed in 'twee' fancy dress kilt regalia, complete with red-haired tartan bonnets, ready for battle. They were all shouting a William Wallace war cry from the film 'Braveheart.' It was an eye-opening moment for everyone standing on the pier. As it was very inclement weather, we were all dressed sensibly in storm gear and rolling our eyes.

The eccentric and very loud tourist ran forward. I was praying to the Norse gods that he wasn't part of my tour party.

Unfortunately, he choose me to approach and abruptly demanded to know where the castle was, to which I responded, “Balfour Castle is on the island of Shapinsay.” The rude individual jeered at me, demanding,

“Hey you, I want Edinburgh Castle. Where is it?”

I pulled myself up to my not inconsiderable height, drew a deep breath and replied,

“This is Orkney not Edinburgh. Edinburgh is several hundred miles south of our islands.”

To which the man, confused and embarrassed, asked the question,

“Then why are we dressed like this?”

A fellow passenger, who had been standing and listening to all this, told him that he was a rude idiot and suggested getting back on board and looking at a map. Suffice to say several people gave him and his embarrassed family a round of applause for their fancy dress.

I breathed a sigh of relief that he wasn’t with my tour.

Burray, or is it Barra? - In 2016, I picked up a couple from the Northlink Ferry in Stromness. They wanted to visit their favourite place in Orkney, which they had read about in an American travel guide book. I should have known that it was going to be a long day when the woman who spoke, greeted me in what I think was Scottish Gaelic.

Anyway, as I stood like a rabbit in the headlights, the man said something else in Gaelic. To this, I responded, "We don't speak Gaelic here in the Northern Isles." A look of shock and bewilderment appeared over their faces.

As we drove across the third Churchill Barrier, the couple had a specific request to visit Burray. So we stopped at the lovely Sands Hotel for a tasty lunch. What happened next put me into a state of shock. The man, whom we shall name Bob, asked me where the beach landing strip was. I said we don't have one here and that the closest airfield was on Lamb Holm at the end of Barrier No 1. Bob looked perplexed and showed me a video on YouTube of a small aircraft landing on a beach strip. I looked closely at the location and then, with as much composure as I could muster - which at that point was a herd of Buffalo running through a glass shop - quietly mentioned that this is Burray, a village in the Orkney Islands, not Barra in the Western Isles. Bob looked dumbstruck and exclaimed, "Are you kidding?!"

I then showed show the couple a map indicating where Barra was in relation to Burray. Approximately 350 miles South of us. It's all in the wording, 'Orkney Uncovered'.

After this monumental *faux pas*, the couple burst out laughing and to my great relief had a wonderful day exploring the South Isles of Orkney.

Incidentally, I never found out whether they managed to get to Barra to do the beach landing nor not; I have heard it's a lot of fun!

Burray not Barra!

Southern Hemisphere - Another question I receive regularly is: 'In which direction are we looking?' In 2018 I took a solo traveller from New Zealand on tour, who was adamant that I didn't know my directions. After a few minutes of showing him how the compass worked, I explained that we were in the Northern Hemisphere, not the Southern Hemisphere and whichever way one turns the compass, the pointer will always point north.

Western Isles - On a weekly basis we receive emails from people who mention that they are currently in Lewis and Harris, and could they please come and do a tour of Orkney? To this, we always respond saying that it's not possible, and give a short explanation of where we are geographically located.

On occasion, as a guide, I have to deal with some confrontational characters. The following is a case in point:

Fairly recently I received a call from a family who said they had arrived on the island and could I take them on a tour. I was available, so we agreed on a price and then I asked where they were staying. They answered, 'Glen Kyles.' I said that I hadn't heard of this accommodation and asked in which part of the island was it located. The man abruptly replied, "How can you not know an area in which you live? Obviously you are not the man to do my family's tour!"

I did a quick search and discovered that Glen Kyles was actually on the island of Harris.

After another mini-meltdown from the gentleman in question, I breathed in slowly and patiently asked,

"Are you on the island of Harris?"

The gentleman angrily replied, "Of course we are! What kind of guide are you?"

To which I answered, "One who lives in Orkney, in the Northern Isles, a couple of hundred miles north of Harris."

I continued, “Furthermore, perhaps you should familiarise yourself with something called a map of Scotland.” His anger then turned to embarrassment as he mumbled some sort of an apology before hanging up.

Side notes:

The Churchill Barriers were built in WWII to prevent German U-boats accessing the British Home Fleet anchored at Scapa Flow. On the 14th October 1939 battleship HMS Royal Oak was torpedoed by U-47 in Scapa Flow, with the loss of 835 men on board. As a result, Winston Churchill ordered the immediate construction of four concrete barriers to permanently stop enemy incursions from the East to the North Sea.

We speak English in Orkney. Many locals speak with an Orcadian dialect, which is a version of the English language. Some people can speak Norwegian and Danish, but I personally don’t know a single person here in Orkney who speaks Gaelic. Remember, we were part of Scandinavia until the 15th Century.

Chapter 5

Ancient Orkney

Ancient Orkney is a vast subject in itself. Our islands have been continually inhabited for the last 10,000 years or more. We are very lucky that we have some of the best Neolithic, Bronze Age, Iron Age and Viking sites in the world.

Historic Environment Scotland do a great job of maintaining and managing these important historic sites of interest.

Our Ancient sites from this period mostly date back to the 3rd Millennium BC. If you don't follow the BC dating, then that's around 5000 years ago.

So, you can imagine some of the fascinating questions and amusing quotes that countless people from around the globe have asked the Rangers from Historical Environmental Scotland and numerous guides, including myself. I will break these down into categories to make it easier to read. Enjoy!

Maeshowe Chambered Cairn – 5000 year old tomb

Great Granddaddy – (I would first add that this has no reference to the American indie rock band called Granddaddy, in California.)

One of my most challenging tours was with a family who had booked a private tour to explore their genealogy. The family, who had apparently done their DNA tests, had one goal on their trip: to discover Maeshowe, as they had learned about its history by speaking to their friends.

We arrived for our tour of Maeshowe with our Historical Environmental Scotland guide and me as their private guide. On the way to the tomb, one of the children mentioned that they couldn't wait to see where their 'Great Granddaddy' was buried. I called in a quick family huddle and mentioned that the tomb had been empty when it was uncovered in 1861. The father said that I didn't know what I was talking about, so I simply called over the other guide, who also explained that the tomb was 5000 years old and the last people who were believed to have used it were Norse raiders in approximately 1153.

The family said that they had come a long way to see where said 'Great Granddaddy' was laid to rest. I explained that there were empty chambers and lots of amazing runic writing for the children.

The tour went well, and as we exited the chambered tomb the father said, and I quote,

"We are very disappointed: someone must have taken his body out as a grave robber."

Again, I said the information he had received was not accurate. The children, meanwhile, were great, they asked loads of amazing questions about the runes and were chuffed to see the runic drawings.

We approached the tour vehicle in haste, the father pulling out his rucksack and forcefully handing me the map and information of 'Great Granddaddy's burial. I looked at the ruffled papers and noticed that it said Maidstone. It took all my effort to remain cool. I simply took a deep breath and quietly and calmy explained that Maidstone is a town in England approx. 745 miles south of Orkney. The father looked blankly at me.

I informed him, "You are in the far northern reaches of Scotland. Not only is this tomb not called Maidstone, you are also in the wrong country."

At this point his wife, who had been calm and polite, burst out laughing and gave her husband a sarcastic round of applause, before deeply apologising for his behaviour.

The rest of the tour went swimmingly and the family had a great time visiting the ancient sites while the father sat in the vehicle in a huff.

I do hope that the family managed to find 'Great Granddaddy's grave while visiting the charming English town of Maidstone in Kent.

1000 years – In late summer 2017 I took a couple from the far reaches of South America on their tour. I picked them up from their ship and whisked them off on their ancient adventure. Our first stop was Maeshowe. It was a bright, warm day and they commented on how wonderful the air was.

As we walked towards the site I explained about our ancient history. The couple stopped me immediately and said that they only believe that the world is 1000 years old, and they didn't wish to discuss this further. (I should add that it states clearly on our website that we will visit ancient structures of around 5000 years old, but they had booked anyway.)

This was by far and away one of the hardest tours I have done, as the clients corrected me on every site. Maeshowe was especially memorable, because even after the guide had explained its age and Neolithic builders, they asked which metal swords did the ancients use to kill each other before being placed in the (1000 year old tomb). I replied, "It was the Stone Age, therefore, there was no metal for making swords." The gentleman then commented that it wasn't Stone Age but Norse, because of the Runic Writing. I laughed and said his theory was inaccurate, as the year was 2017 and the fall of the Vikings was 1066 AD. The distance in time is 951 years. The Viking Ages did not last for a mere 49 years longer than this date, but hundreds of years longer.

We continued the tour, but as we walked back to the tour vehicle, the gentleman said that he was considered to be an expert in Viking history by his peers, and through his research - taken from the T.V. series 'Vikings' – he knew that the Great Ragnar Lothbrok was the first conqueror of the world at that time. To which I pointed out that Ragnar was born in the 9th Century, before his son Ivar the Boneless led an invasion of East Anglia in England in 865 AD. Smugly, the gentleman commented, "I know, isn't it great?"

I pointed out that his theory of Earth being 1000 years old was blown out of the water as Ragnar was born around 1200 years ago.

He pondered this for a moment and then agreed that his information must be inaccurate. I then had a great time explaining the Yesnaby cliffs and the geology of Orkney dating back to 400 million years ago.

Naked Chant – In 2021 I met a group of ladies from the ferry terminal in Stromness. They had booked a private tour of the ancient sites.

We stopped for our scheduled tour of Maeshowe Chambered Tomb, and as we arrived there, I noticed that two of the four women had on long towels and a jacket. I said that they should be wearing more clothing, as it was cold and wet outside the vehicle. One of the group said that they wanted to dance naked inside the tomb, while the others chanted....

A look of horror swept across my face, followed by bewilderment. I calmy told them, "No I am sorry but you cannot do this, as it's indecent exposure and you will likely be arrested. Furthermore, there will be a number of other people, including children, on the tour." The women agreed that perhaps they hadn't thought this through and they would come back in the future and visit when it is dark. I remember thinking - *good luck, as it is locked at night!*

Standing Stones of Stenness and the Ring of Brodgar

These two foreboding Henge monuments are very visible and popular with locals and visitors alike. We walk our yellow labrador, Holly, the long way around the Ring of Brodgar, passing by the brackish loch of Stenness and freshwater loch of Harray. From any of the hillsides that surround the lochs you can clearly make out these impressive stone circles.

They predate the more commonly known Stone Henge in Wiltshire by around several hundred years. From what we know about these ancient people, it is believed that ancient people settled in Orkney first, before making their way South. There was a National Geographic edition called Britain's Ancient Capital, which is worth a read. I may not be an Archaeologist by trade but I am well versed. Without further ado, here are some classic questions I have been asked about these stone megaliths.

No, it's not Outlander – one of the most annoying things that anyone who lives in Orkney can witness, is people hugging the 20ft high Standing Stones, quoting some line in Gaelic from the series 'Outlander'.

This popular series of books and follow-up TV show by Starz, with the dashing 18th Century soldier, Jamie, and the lovestruck WW II nurse, Claire, has proved very popular but for many of us Scots it is a double-edged sword. On one side it's been phenomenal for Scottish tourism, on the other side it's now a constant battle trying to politely educate the fans who visit Orkney that 'Outlander' is the work of fiction, not real like the Orkney Sea Haggis.

A few years back I was at the Stones of Stenness having a walk and taking photographs. I suddenly heard a loud Scottish accent and looked around to see a guide from outwith Orkney, in full swing with his arms flapping and his kilt flying. The man, who was guiding two Spanish women, said, "And this is where Claire touched the stone and was transformed back to the 18th Century, to see her Jamie." The two women looked very sceptical and dismissive. As I pretended to take pictures, I was actually listening to this man and his epic BAFTA-winning performance. All credit to him, he was engaging.

However, a local man, who had also been listening to his performance, approached him and said these exact words:

"What a load of bollocks! 'Outlander' is fictitious! This is Orkney, not Inverness. These are actual stones, not Styrofoam like the fake 'Outlander' stones. Get your facts right, you dafty!"

As the women gave the local a round of applause, the man in the kilt glared at him. I kept on walking with a slight smile.

In fairness to the guide he was a great actor, perhaps he can contact Starz for a role on the show.

This Standing Stone is not, I repeat **not,** ***made of Styrofoam.***

Battle of the Standing Stones – More commonly than not, visitors to the islands love to try and take selfies with farm and wild animals. This, as you can imagine, does not always go according to plan.

In the summer of 2018 I witnessed a group of people walking across the Henge at the Standing Stones of Stenness, towards a number of what they *thought* were sheep. I shouted across to them to warn them that they were in fact rams, but they chose not to heed my advice - to their peril.

As they approached for their selfies, I could see the rams starting to get riled. As my private group and I backed cautiously out of the site, we saw what could only be described as the Charge of the Light Brigade. Instead of British cavalry vs Russian artillery at the Battle of Balaclava, it was Orkney Rams vs Selfie Squad. There were screams and panic from the Selfie Squad as the rams went on a head-butting rampage. One individual even tried to do a selfie video of a ram charging towards him!

Still to this day, I am not sure what went through his mind as he was butted to the ground. I think it's the most fun the rams had enjoyed since being allowed in with their ewes for mating. They charged from one side of the Henge to the other. Everyone else who was outside the site was laughing, clapping and heckling the Selfie Squad, who manged to limp out of the Stone Circle covered in sheep poo, mud and shame. As we walked back to the vehicle my clients were crying with laughter. They said in a later email that the Battle of the Standing Stones had been the highlight of their trip.

Beware: If you see a Ram charging towards you with intent, high-tail it out of the field pronto. They are not called Rams for nothing!

The iPad Scandal - In 2014 I took a lovely couple from Japan on tour around the ancient sites. Throughout the entire tour the lady was using her iPad to take pics. I did mention that she would get a better view with her own eyes and without the use of modern technology.

The lady, whom we shall call Karen, was blissfully unaware that wearing dark polarised sunglasses may obscure her view through the iPad in question. Anyway, at our last stop, the Standing Stones of Stenness, she screamed and threw her iPad to the ground in a fit of rage and said something in rapid Japanese. I asked her husband what she had said and he replied,

"My wife had her iPad camera in selfie mode and has taken selfies all day."

It took every ounce of my being not to burst into tears of laughter. Karen's husband's laughter echoed around the Henge.

Flash and Dash – You may remember in a previous story about a group of ladies whom I took on tour in 2021. This same group after deciding to abandon their naked chant ideas at Maeshowe, then decided to randomly flash at the Ring of Brodgar.

As we walked around the massive Henge Monument, I sensed that I was walking ahead of the group and turned around to see three of them had stripped to their undies and were attempting to shield themselves from the eyes of many other people who were also walking around Henge. One of the ladies was shivering and muttering some humming chant, whilst trying to hug a Stone. I ran over to them and insisted that they immediately get up and put their clothes back on, as the only energy they would feel was hypothermia. That or a cold police cell for indecent exposure.

Luckily, they came to their senses, re-donned their clothes and I marched them out of the stone circle past a small jeering mob who had gathered to take pictures. Flash and dash over, thank heavens. There was silence in the vehicle under a cloud of embarrassment until we arrived at Waulkmill Bay for a picnic. The weather had cleared and it was nice and sunny. "Perfect for a sea swim" one of them shouted as they all ran into the sea and left me holding their towels and various items of clothing like a giant clothes horse!

The Minefield – During the Second World War anti-invasion training took place in various parts of Orkney, including the Ring of Brodgar. It always makes me laugh when I think how kind of ancient man to dig out a big circular ditch to allow the British Army access thousands of years later. There is a famous photo from the Imperial War Museum that shows the 9th Battalion Gordon Highlanders in 1941 driving through the Henge with their universal carriers. Since the World Wars, people have been finding all sorts of unexploded ordnance (UXO) around the islands and my brothers in the Royal Navy Bomb Disposal are up here regularly making the islands safe.

The Ring of Brodgar centre is restricted and visitors are asked to stick to the designated paths, but there is always some diehard who deliberately ignores the 'Stick to the path' signs and triumphantly marches into the centre. A couple of years back, I was walking around the ring with my yellow Labrador, Holly, when I noticed a group of people ignoring the signs and heading into the middle. There were several other people respectfully following the rules and looking on in disgust.

I just couldn't help myself and stopped walking. I shouted out to the group, "Hey I wouldn't go in there if I were you!"

The group looked back and one person shouted out,

"What the heck are you going to do about it!" To which I jokingly replied,

"Oh, I am not bothered about you ignoring the signs and entering the centre, but the military heavily used this area during the War and there may be mines, grenades and other unexploded ordnance under your feet, so be careful."

I turned round and kept walking with wee Holly in tow.

As I glanced back, I heard some expletives amongst the group as they gingerly tried to double back as gently as they could muster. A lovely family walked past me and asked if there were unexploded bombs, to which I answered no. I merely wanted to see their reaction. The family burst out laughing and gave a loud round of applause and some heckling to the dafties cautiously making their way out.

Where is the circle? – In 2015 I was guiding a charming couple around the Ring of Brodgar. It was a beautifully warm summers day and while we walked and talked about the the marvel ahead of us and listened to the skylarks high above us, our peace and quiet was shattered by a very noisy tourist running towards us, hair flying and hands flapping. The lady who looked like she had been dragged through a hedge backwards was fuming about how her time had been wasted. I asked her politely if she was ok and needed some help. The lady angrily responded, "Are you one of these joker locals, who tell people to visit a Stone Circle that doesn't exist?"

I looked stunned and then patiently answered,

"You are in a Stone Circle."

The lady snapped, '"Where is the Circle, I have been walking for ages looking for it!"

I told her that she had walked around it. I literally had to show her a picture of the Ring of Brodgar from the sky to show her the Circle. No thank you was offered by the lady in question.

She simply answered, "Well how stupid of the builders to make it so difficult for us to walk around it. They should have signposted it better!"

My clients and I looked at each other dumbstruck and with a slight smirk kept walking.

Look a Meerkat – Last year I saw a group of people standing near the path overlooking the Ring of Brodgar and frantically taking pictures of what they thought was a Meerkat. As I slowly edged by the gathering masses, I saw two Stoats, which are an invasive species to Orkney, playing on a stone. They were darting about and refusing to stand still for the numerous amateur photographers. I very politely told the gathered group that they were Stoats, not Meerkats. Several of them took some super shots of the wee beasties and I commended them on their valiant efforts.

Skara Brae

The remains of this once thriving 5000 year old Neolithic village was discovered under sand dunes by a massive storm in November 1850. It is an incredible site to behold and commands an imposing view over the North Atlantic. Skara Brae as it is known is one of the oldest and best preserved villages in North West Europe. Coastal erosion, rising seas and perhaps natural events such as Tsunamis have taken away a large section of the village.

The long walk – On my first week of trading, I had heard from members of the Skara Brae staff that they heard some absolute classics for random questions. As I was taking a picture for my client while at the site, a visitor interrupted me and asked if there was a car to take him back to the visitor centre. I said that the walk back from the Stone Age village to the centre would take no more than about 5 minutes. To which he responded, "Why on earth did the ancients build the village so far from the road?"

Powering Skara Brae – Having explained fully to a small tour group that the houses were made of stone, and there was no metal tools involved with the construction, one of the group then asked me how did they then get electricity to the 5000 year old village!

My Great Uncle is from Skara Brae – In 2014 I took a family from a visiting cruise ship to Skara Brae as part of their ancient tour. The matriarch of the family had specifically asked to visit Skara Brae as she wanted to see where her Great Uncle was from. I actually thought she meant the area which is Skaill. As we walked down to the site, having seen the short four minute video explaining its discovery in a powerful storm in 1850, the matriarch excitedly exclaimed, "I can't believe we have arrived." She pointed to the ancient buildings and continued, "I am surprised at how small the house is where my Great Uncle lived."

At this point I mentioned that she was mistaken and that the last residents were the Neolithic people over 5000 years ago. The matriarch then proceeded to tell her children that their guide was incorrect and that they had travelled across the North Atlantic for nothing. Holding my tongue, I called over to one of the site staff, who was very happy to corroborate my accurate information. He informed the lady in question that perhaps she'd simply got her facts wrong and should listen to her expert guide.

In fairness to the matriarch, one of her friends had given her incorrect information and without doing her own research had decided to push on ahead and book a private tour.

Halt! Mein Bratwurst – By far one of the funniest things I have witnessed while at Skara Brae, was when I was walking along the path to the site with my clients. It was a warm summers day in 2017 with plenty of blue sky and a few marauding herring gulls looking for snacks from the unsuspecting visitors. As we stopped to talk about the weather, there was a sudden swoosh from an aerial combatant. This ballsy herring gull swooped out of the heavens at lightning speed and pinched an unsuspecting German man's sausage.

"Halt! Mein Bratwurst," could be heard echoing across Skaill Bay. To make matters worse the herring gull clearly didn't like the look of the man's sausage and dropped it into the sea, before flying off to find another victim with a tastier snack.

"Schweinhund," the man shouted whilst waving his fists angrily. My clients and I plus numerous people who had witnessed this snatch and grab burst out laughing. The poor German man had to resort to heavily guarding his back up sandwich while taking quick bites.

Gulls are not partial to Bratwurst sausages.

Other hilarious questions from Skara Brae visitors:

Is this where the Hobbit was filmed?

Did the ancients have access to a cinema?

Is this where the children's TV series Teletubbies was filmed?

Can we play hide and seek in the old houses?

Please can my children light a fire in the old houses?

Can we meet the ancient people?

Can we visit the food shop that the ancients used?

Can we camp here overnight?

Does Skara Brae take accommodation booking?

Chapter 6

Orkney WILD life

Puffins - where are the puffins? Puffins are known as the Tammie Norrie here in Orkney. You tend to see them between the months of May and July, but they are not everywhere as global warming has lessened their food supply. Presently, the best island in which to see them is Westray at Castle O'Burrian where there are literally thousands of them.

Puffin Stalking - A couple of years back you can imagine my surprise when a chap from the Southern Hemisphere asked to see the elusive Puffin in September. I did explain that Mr and Mrs Puffin with their Pufflings will be now back to sea.

This chap was determined to spot them and throughout his private tour kept asking if there is a chance, he might see them. To which the answer from me was always, "That's highly unlikely." Anyway, he decided to buy a soft toy Puffin and have me place said Puffin on the cliffs with a bit of seaweed around it. Indeed! I then suggested that he use a photo of a puffin and superimpose it on to an Orkney scenic background. The penny dropped. But that was indeed what he did.

Puffin to the left, Toy Puffin to the right.

No Puffin - Then there was the time I was asked by a family if I could whistle to a Puffin and they could take it home with them. They had even brought a small cage and bedding. I looked skywards hoping the mighty Thor might strike me down. I calmly explained to the children that they are notoriously hard to corral, fast and agile and like unicorns they live freely. Luckily that was acceptable and their net and cage were left in the vehicle.

Puffin Keep - In summer 2019 I was sitting on a warm

day outside St Magnus Cathedral enjoying an Orkney ice cream with my young son Benjamin. As we talked about all things Super Mario Bros and Sonic the Hedgehog, I noticed that the sun had suddenly been blanked out by a very large visitor from a cruise ship. He was red in the face and dripping in sweat. He proceeded to bark something at us in unintelligible English.

Translated to: *Where are the darn puffins at?*

I told him bluntly to leave us alone and not be so rude in front of my son and I. He barked again, "Where are they!"

I stood up and pointed to the Puffin Keep (the Moosie Toor), at the top of the Bishops Palace and accessible only by a high, spiral, stone cut, narrow staircase. The man didn't thank me and stormed off.

Finishing our ice creams, Benjamin and I walked around the side of the Cathedral. We waited....Suddenly there was a burst of more unintelligible English with some swearing. I put my hands over my son's ears. The rude man stared down at us from the top of the Bishop's Palace as we waved back at him, happy that we had sent him on a mythical adventure. Had the man in question been polite I would have told him where to look for Puffins on a coastal walk.

Haggis Hibernation – Now the Haggis, although lovely little creatures of mystery and intrigue, do like to be left in peace and are known for their territorial disputes between other Haggis. So, you can imagine how candidly I had to approach a question fielded from a young man who was convinced that a group of Haggis lived in the centre of the Ring of Brodgar.

I politely asked the young man who had told him about the fearsome Brodgar Haggis. The child pointed to his Mum and Dad, who were both doing their very best to remain calm and keep the legend of the Brodgar Haggis going.

There was a rustle amongst the heather beside the stone circle and I said to the young man that it was the family of Brodgar Haggii: Adult Haggis; junior Haglets and baby Mealie Pudding. By this time a group of others had gathered by and were intently listening to my story and looking for the mythical creatures. To quietly put the matter to rest I told the young man and many gatherers that the family of Haggis were highly camouflaged and bedding down for hibernation, as it was the summer months in which they hibernate not the winter. The young man who seemed happy with this explanation thanked me and we continued the tour, much to his parents relief. I do wonder what the group of ten visitors thought as we left.

The family of Brodgar Haggis hiding in the heather? Spot the adult Haggis, the junior Haglets and the baby Mealie Pudding.

Bonxie Bombardment – One of the most feared birds in Orkney for many a hill walker is the Great Skua, or rather Bonxie as it is more commonly known in the UK. This large sea bird is brown/grey in colour, with black feet, black eyes, black beak and white wingtips. The locals say that if you see the white wing tips it's too late for you, as they swoop down out of the heavens like Stuka dive bombers and bonk you on the back of your head with their bellies. They are formidable aerial apex predators that fly in pairs and attack sea birds for their eggs and for sport. For anyone who reads this, please note that they spend more time in heathery fields and valleys than they do on the cliffs, so beware if you decided to take a shortcut. These well camouflaged birds mostly live on the island of Hoy in their thousands, but can be seen throughout Orkney.

In the Summer of 2018 I took a lovely couple on the Old Man of Hoy sea stack walk, approximately 7.6 km round trip over moderate terrain. As we reached the last part of the plateau walk to the 450ft high sea stack, the husband sheepishly approached me and asked if there was somewhere he could go to the toilet. (Imagine barren landscape, with heather, rocks and sea cliffs). To which I answered, "As you can see there are no toilets, just the great outdoors." The man answered that was fine but he needed a number two. His wife and I gave him what scraps of tissues we had and wished him luck on his intrepid journey to relieve himself near a non-descript stone. We turned our backs so the man could be at peace with nature. That was short lived when we heard screams combined with panic. The man in question had gone off-piste and decided to sit in the heather and unknown to him, right in the middle of a large scale Bonxie nesting ground.

I tried my best to shout to the man that he needed to leave the area immediately. Squadron after squadron of Bonxie flew towards their bare arsed target. The man managed to pull up his trousers while under Bonxie bombardment and in a futile attempt threw torn bits of heather towards the aerial assailants, which expertly darted past his head intent on more bombardment!

I was aware of hysterical sobs and looked behind me. The man's wife was literally doubled over, crying with laughter, tears rolling down her face as she tried to video her dishevelled husband, making his way past the fierce aerial assault of marauding Bonxies.

As the man reached the trail and the Bonxies backed off, his wife simply said, "I hope you washed your hands."

Unicorn lair – Many of my tours are tailored for families to enjoy, with many mini adventurers wanting to hear fascinating snippets about all sorts of interesting creatures on Orkney.

In June 2022 I picked up a delightful family from a Disney Cruise Ship. The youngest daughter had a fascination about Scotland's National Animal, the fabled Unicorn. When we arrived at Skara Brae, I did an alternative tour geared completely to her and her siblings.

The tour started from when we walked on to the path and headed to the Unicorn lair. I carefully showed the children the areas in which for hundreds of years Unicorns populated Orkney and the local people here from the Neolithic period helped nurture them.

Since the discovery of the Unicorn lair, much has been learned about the way these precious, fabled animals lived, ate, slept, laughed and cried. So, in depth, I explained about their central meeting place in Structure 1 and their workshop in Structure 8, where they made beautiful straw tied harnesses for the Unicorns. The children asked where they had disappeared to. I explained that because the sea levels were rising and the Ancient People found it difficult to live and look after their precious Unicorns. The herd then decided to head off to the mountains of Mainland Scotland and over thousands of years some lucky people still spot the Unicorns in the mountains or taking a drink of fresh mountain spring water, to ensure their powers remain strong.

I did the entire Ancient Tour Day based on the Unicorns of Orkney. The parents said that it was an incredible and informative tour which I had engineered to perfection with their children in mind. While learning about the Unicorns and their habitat, they gained an insight into the Ancient People of Orkney. In their 5 stars review they said that it had been the highlight of their entire Disney trip and their children spoke about wanting to return to Orkney to discover more fascinating places and creatures.

For me it was great as I did a similar tour with my son Benjamin when he was three years old and it brought back many happy memories. One of the reasons I wrote this book was so my son can look back in years to come and enjoy reading about some of his dad's hilarious anecdotes and also some testing times in - Adventures of Orkney Uncovered.

With Thanks...

My wife Kirsty and my son Benajmin for their unwavering patience and persistence in pushing me to finish this book.

My mum and dad for telling me to keep calm and carry on. This is harder than one might think, particularly with my fiery Viking bloodline ☺.

Commander Keith Mabbott Royal Navy (Rtd). Mabbs as he is more commonly known is a great friend who loves the outdoors. Mabbs served his country for many years and it is my honour to have him write the foreword to this book.

Liz Fraser – One of the UK's best known writers and broadcasters on aspects of family life and travel. Liz very kindly helped edit the book and provided some excellent feedback.

Julie Miller – The designer of all things Orkney Uncovered merchandise. Thanks to Julie's skill set we have countless people throughout the world proudly wearing our Orkney Uncovered gear. Julie is an amazingly talented artist. Please do check out her website.

Margaret Amatt – without whose help and guidance this book might never have made it to publication.

And finally to all my family, friends and tens of thousands of loyal followers, thank you for your unwavering support in following my Adventures with Orkney Uncovered.

Special Mention:

I would like to give a special mention to the Royal Navy Diving & Threat Exploitation Group (DTXG), formerly Fleet Diving Squadron (FDS). It is an honour to be a loyal servant and part of their brotherhood.

I have a huge amount of respect for the Explosive Ordnance Disposal (EOD) Community and the hard work with extreme danger they deal with throughout the world to keep us safe. In 2021 the Northern Diving Group was awarded the Freedom of Orkney. For over 40 years DTXG teams have safely disposed of wartime ordnance that has washed up on the Orkney coastline.

I actively support the Felix Fund Charity, who aim to assist with the well-being of individuals within the EOD and Search Community across all British Military. Therefore, I will be donating 20% of any profits of this book to them.

VIRTUS IN ALTUM-VIRES IN ATRUM

Strength in the Deep, Strength in the Dark.

Key

Neo = New.

Lithic = Stone.

Neolithic = New Stone Age.

SB = Skara Brae.

BC = Before Christ.

AD = Anno Domini.

Sq. mi = Square miles.

Mph = Miles per hour

Btn = Battalion.

RN = Royal Navy.

HES = Historic Environment Scotland.

UXO = Unexploded Ordnance.

EOD = Explosive Ordnance Disposal.

Henge = ditch or a rampart that surrounds a stone or wooden structure used for ceremonial purpose.

Half inched = Pinched, took without permission.

Huff = Annoyance, sulk.

Printed in Great Britain
by Amazon

48329293R00046